The New Vestments

by **Edward Lear**   Illustrated by **DeLoss McGraw**

SIMON & SCHUSTER BOOKS FOR YOUNG READERS

For
my wonderful
childhood and those
responsible: Mom, Gram, Grandad,
Ray, Fount, Curtis, Jimmie and Doc, the
Noble elementary teachers, Mrs. Anderson, Mrs.
Lovelady, Mrs. McKinney and her little store, Gibb and his
market, the police, the barbers, the doctors, the churches,
Mrs. Cox, Don, Betty, Stanton, Jim, Lloyd, Tommy, Nokey,
Bobby, Billy, Jon, Ricky, Mark, Jimmy, Freddy, Gene, the
girls — Janie, Jeannie, Alice, Ellen, Kathy, Mary, Diana,
Judy, Patty, Kaye — the soda jerks, the mean boys in the
East End, the boys standing in front of pool halls, Friday
night football games, a million cats, and all the dogs that
chased me — D. M.

SIMON & SCHUSTER BOOKS FOR YOUNG READERS
An imprint of Simon & Schuster Children's Publishing Division
1230 Avenue of the Americas, New York, New York 10020
Illustrations copyright © 1995 by DeLoss McGraw
SIMON & SCHUSTER BOOKS FOR YOUNG READERS
is a trademark of Simon & Schuster.
Book design by Joy Chu
The text for this book is set in 27-point Antique Olive Bold.
The illustrations were done in gouache.
Manufactured in the United States of America
10 9 8 7 6 5 4 3 2 1

Library of Congress Cataloging-in-Publication Data
Lear, Edward, 1812 – 1888.
The new vestments / by Edward Lear ;
illustrated by DeLoss McGraw.
p. cm.
Summary: The town fool discovers that, while a suit made
of pork chops, pancakes, dead mice, and similar materials
is unusual, it has definite disadvantages.
1. Nonsense verses, English.   2. Children's poetry, English.
[1. Clothing and dress — Poetry.   2. Nonsense verse.
3. English poetry.]   I. McGraw, DeLoss, ill.   II. Title.
PR4879.L2N27   1995 821' .8 — dc20   94-16713   CIP   AC
ISBN: 0-671-50089-9

There lived an Old Man in the Kingdom of Tess,

Who invented a purely original dress;
And when it was perfectly made
and complete,

He opened the door, and walked into

the street.

By way of a hat, he'd a loaf of Brown Bread,
In the middle of which he inserted his head;

His Shirt was made up of no end of dead Mice,

The warmth of whose skins was quite fluffy and nice;

His drawers were of Rabbit-skins; so were his Shoes—

His Stockings were skins—but it is not known whose

His Waistcoat and Trowsers were made of Pork Chops;

His Buttons were Jujubes, and Chocolate Drops;

His Coat was all Pancakes with Jam for a border,
And a girdle of Biscuits to keep it in order;

And he wore over all, as a screen from bad

A cloak of green Cabbage-leaves stitched

He had walked

weather;

all together.

a short way, when he heard a great noise,

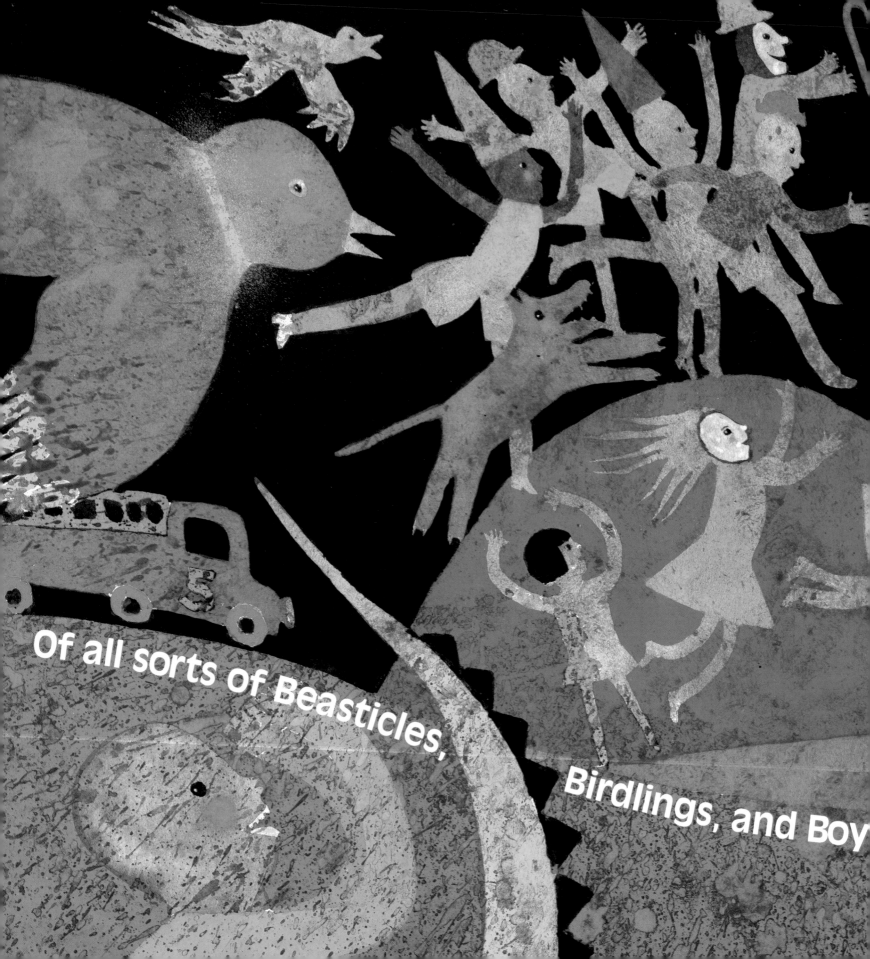

Of all sorts of Beasticles,

Birdlings, and Boy

And from every long street and dark lane in the town Beasts, Birdles, and Boys in a tumult rushed down.

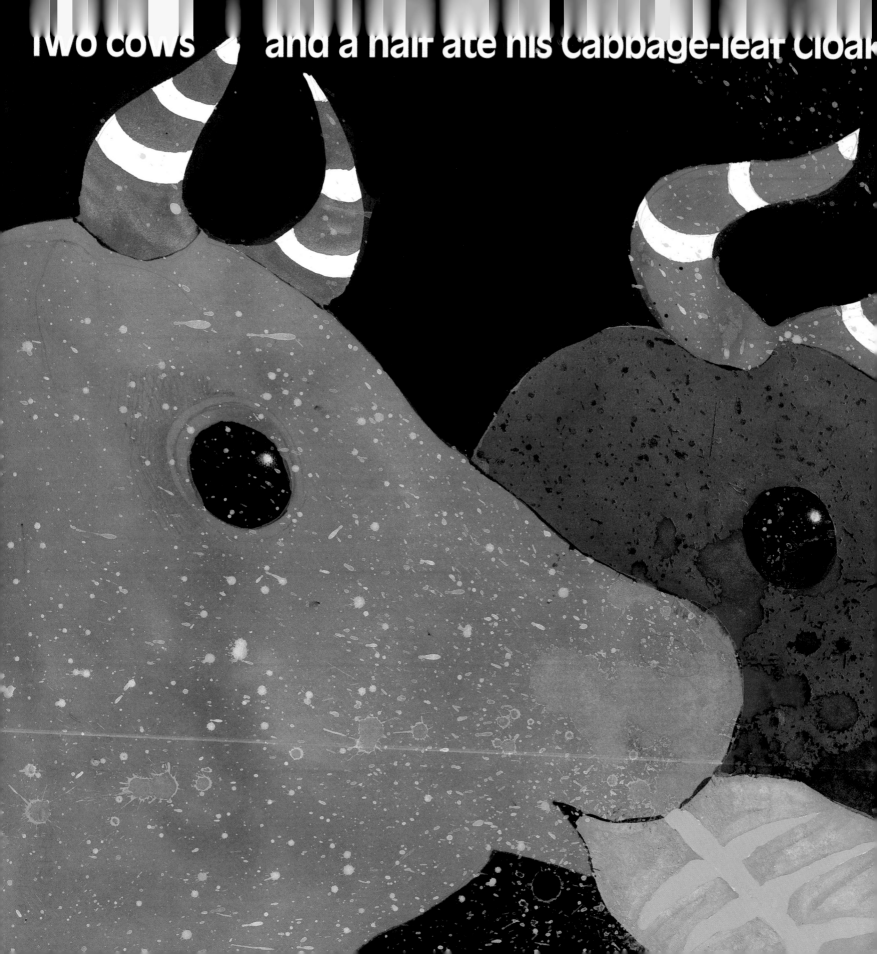
Two cows and a half ate his Cabbage-leaf Cloak

Four Apes seized his Girdle, which vanished like smoke;

Three Kids ate up half of his Pancakey Coat, and the

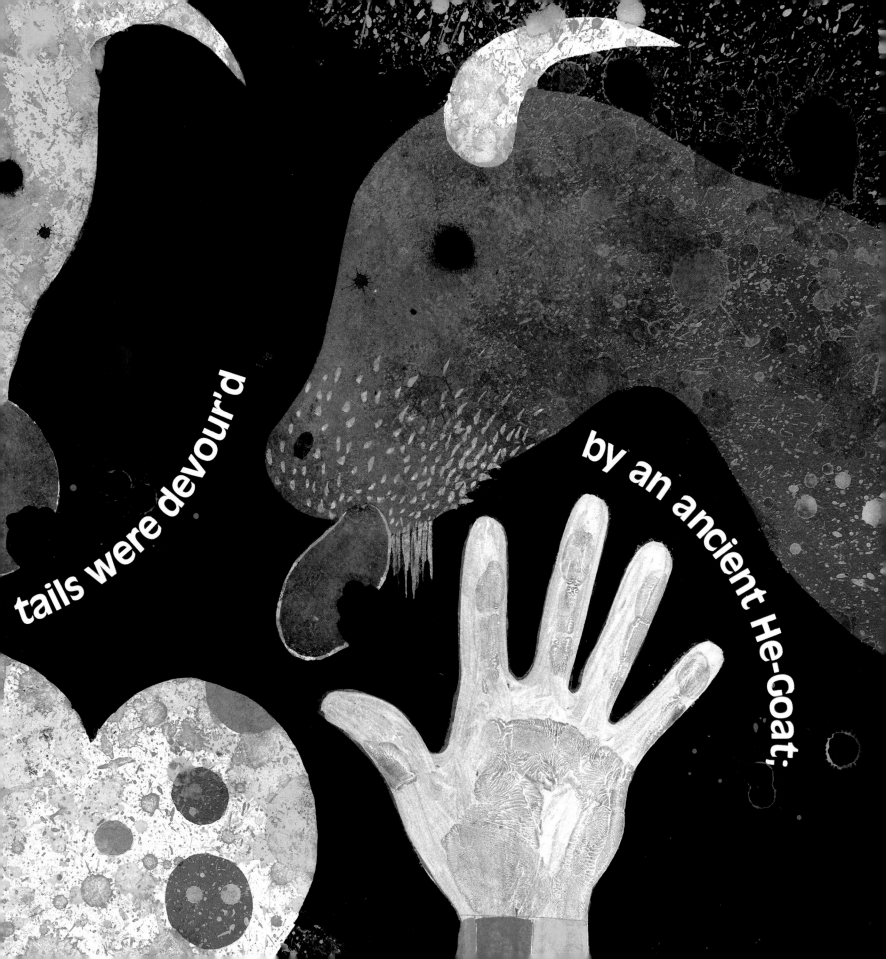

tails were devour'd

by an ancient He-Goat;

Waistcoat and Trowsers to give to their Puppies;

And while they were growling,

and mumbling the Chops,

Ten Boys prigged the Jujubes and Chocolate Drops.

He tried to run back to his house, but in vain,

For scores of fat Pigs came again and again;

They rushed out of stables and novels and doors,

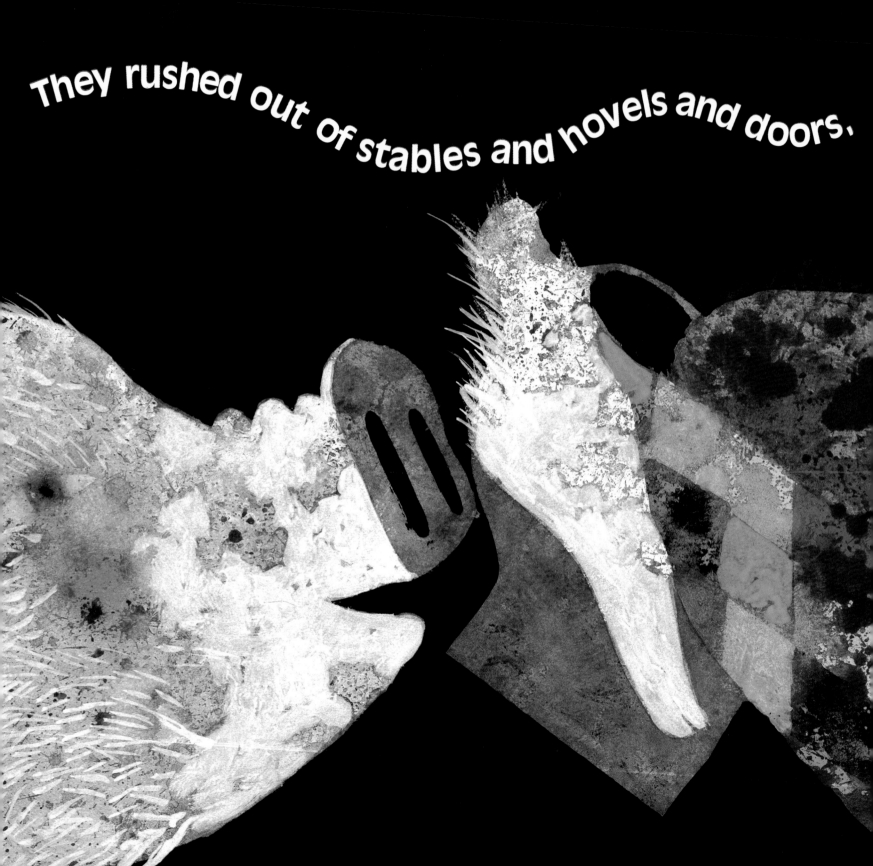

They tore off his stockings, his shoes, and his drawers.

And now from the housetops with screechings descend

striped, spotted, white, black, and gray Cats without end.

They jumped on his shoulders and knocked off his hat,

When Crows, Ducks, and Hens made a mincemeat of that:

They speedily flew at his sleeves in a trice,

And utterly tore up his shirt of dead Mice;

They swallowed the last of his Shirt with a squall,

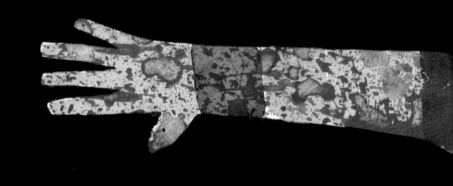

whereon he ran home with no clothes on at all.

And he said to himself as he bolted the door,
"I will not wear a similar dress any more,
Any more, any more, any more, never more!"